DARK ENERGY

DARK ENERGY

Frederick Feirstein

GROLIER ESTABLISHED POETS SERIES
Cambridge, Massachusetts

Composed in Adobe Garamond Pro with Cronos Pro display at Hobblebush Books (www.hobblebush.com)

Printed in the United States of America

ISBN: 978-0-9889352-0-4

Cover art: *Passengers*, painting by Steven Assael

GROLIER SERIES OF ESTABLISHED POETS

Grolier Poetry Book Shop
6 Plympton Street
Cambridge MA 02138

www.grolierpoetrybookshop.org

For Linda, David and Erin Feirstein

CONTENTS

FOREWORD   ix

PART I / GRAVITY OF THE BLACK HOLE

Prologue: Disney on Parade   3

1. Oedipus / Christ / Dionysus   5
Myths   7
Laius   8
The Witch   9
Daydreaming   10
Sinister   11
Gravity of the Black Hole   12

2. Snow White / Sleeping Beauty / Cinderella   13
Fairytales   15
The Prince Finds Sleep   16
Snow White   17
The Prince   18
The Space Dwarf's Advice   20
The Eros Dwarf   21
The Bitter Dwarf   22
The Schizoid Dwarf   23
Pigs   24
Mice   25
Cinderella   26
Ashes   27
The Prince's Father   28
Cinderella's Prince   29
Stepsisters   30
The Prince and Cinderella: The Ending   31

3. Hansel & Gretel / Little Red Riding Hood   33
Caretaking   35
The Gingerbread Witch   36

Hansel's Abandonment   37

Gretel's Mom   38

Hansel And Gretel's Father   39

The Father Says   40

The Stepmom   41

Hansel and Gretel   42

Not a Fairytale   44

A Happy Ending   45

Another Ending   46

The Wolf's Invitation   47

Little Red Riding Hood's Breakdown   48

Little Red Riding Hood's Mother   49

Wolf Philosophy   50

Trümmelbach   51

Epilogue   52

PART 2 / THE TWO SIDES OF THE MOON

Spring   55

The Widow   56

What Happened   57

The House We Had To Sell   59

Three Dimensions   60

Fully Alive   61

Shakespeare   63

The Doctor   64

Red Cross   65

The Pond   66

Oasis   67

Immortal Verse   68

Apology for Dark Energy   69

As Time Goes By   70

Delacorte's Clock   71

Toy Story   73

The Miracle of Ordinary Life   74

FOREWORD

I FIRST MET FREDERICK FEIRSTEIN more than forty years ago during the agony of the Biafran war. Fred was an active member of the American Committee to Keep Biafra Alive and I was a young graduate student in New York City, born in that affected part of the world. This Igbo speaking area of Nigeria's eastern region saw much by way of suffering. Fred and I became friends because of Biafra, and have developed a keen literary association over the years. In a way, this publication of *Dark Energy* by the Grolier Poetry Press, a press which I now direct, marks a journey that has come full circle. My foreword, or introduction, herewith appended, is perhaps superfluous given that I cannot possibly add anything meaningful to the wise and insightful words of X. J. Kennedy, Molly Peacock and Clark Blaise appearing on the back cover of this book. There is a saying in Igboland, *Onye jelu ije, ga ana*— "he that goes on a journey will sooner or later return." *Dark Energy* and its publication is, for both Feirstein and myself, a homecoming of sorts. Readers of Feirstein's dazzling earlier work, *Manhattan Carnival*, already know what to expect from the pen of this master craftsman. Call it a sense of playful defiance in the face of things continuously, profoundly sad. Or call it by some other name. But I venture to observe that for me there is in Fred's work something somewhat sacramental. The poet having seen with clarity, albeit a burdened clarity, a thing or two about the unsettled nature of our situation, (things that are not always clear to the rest of us) has tried to come to terms with this unsettledness through his writing, and through his work as a therapist.

In the hustle and bustle of our disheveled metropolitan centers, and in the deadening sameness of the hinterland, the game of the spirit still goes on. Today, it can be said that with the loss of faith in Heaven, and an attendant parsimony in the cultivation of grace, no one appears to know, any longer, where to turn in the matter of life's meaning. If only this inability could relieve or set one free from the burden of establishing sense, given that everything is now perpetually up in the air, it would have been nice. But it does not, and the self, frazzled as ever to the core of its unsettled being, continues to grope, often to no avail. What moves the poet is this complexity in the structure of loss—the going forward where what is in front might well turn out to be more perverse than what was behind. And then the question arises: what was the point of one's effort to move forward in the first place? In such situations, where uncertainty appears to govern everything, what does the poet or anyone do?

Imagine an example: a person on the edge, a patient let us say, insists that a radiologist is someone who is an expert on radios, that the rest of the world is mistaken in thinking otherwise. Such a patient, is he necessarily without mental shelter? Perhaps; perhaps not. For is not the demand that there be consistency of some kind in the enumeration of speech, something we can well understand even if it appears utterly inappropriate in the given circumstance? A tweaking of rationalities is often called for, and the poet-therapist, with humor in his veins but sadness in his heart, knows what this is all about. There is healing wisdom in the old words of the human tribes, English not excluded. Feirstein, the healer and maker of words, has given us something to think about even in the midst of all that laughter which he has also given us.

Ifeanyi Menkiti

[Fairytales] have a strange logic, the freedom from the constraints of time and space, and the abrupt and violent action that Freud attributed to the 'primary process,' the kind of thinking that prevails in the unconscious and in childhood.

—ELIZABETH DALTON, "INTRODUCTION AND NOTES"
TO *GRIMM'S FAIRY TALES*

There is a crack in everything/ That's how the light gets in.

—LEONARD COHEN, "ANTHEM," THE FUTURE

. . . The Jew's Beech Tree (1942) by the German Annette Droste-Hulshoff made sure that the older image of the "magical Jews" as a threatening collective present in the Grimms' tales did not vanish from this tradition.

—INTRODUCTION TO ANNA O'S SHORT
STORIES BY RENATE LATIMER

ACKNOWLEDGMENTS

These poems first appeared in:

The Hudson Review: "The Miracle of Ordinary Life"
The Ontario Review: "The Doctor"
The Partisan Review: "The House We Had To Sell"
Poetry: "Spring"
Quarterly Review of Literature: "Disney on Parade," "Myths,"
"Daydreaming," "The Pond"
Story Line Press: " Trümmelbach"
Trinacria: "Fairytales," "The Bitter Dwarf," "The Space Dwarf's
Advice, "Shakespeare"
Word Tech: "As Time Goes By," "Re-reading"

Special thanks to Steven Assael for his graciousness in letting me use his
painting *Passengers*.

I

GRAVITY OF THE BLACK HOLE

An Expressionist Sequence

Prologue

DISNEY ON PARADE

Wheeling down Main Street in technicolor light
Are Disney's heroes, our mythology,
A comfort in the middle of the night.

Mickey Mouse, Minnie, Uncle Donald help.
The children of America are sick
Of war, cultural suicide, and greed.
Snow White, Bambi, Lady and the Tramp,
It's midnight now, help us in our hour of need.

You helped us with the witch's oven and
Her poisoned mushrooms. Goofy, Pluto please.
Those childhood traumas were much worse than these.
Teach us to be courageous and naïve.

1. Oedipus / Christ / Dionysus

MYTHS

Groping for consolation in The Final Stage
So we'll seem less crazy for our childrens' sake,
We make our re-enactments *Tragedies*
Where we're heroic, though we know we're fake.

Or, atheists, start singing of The Soul
Like Yeats, that loony we'd have ridiculed
When younger, braver, realer. Who'd believe
We'd harmonize in his strange singing school?

But, better, there's real comedy to tell
If we can find the insight and the will
To tease ourselves into those tiny hells
Where we, chronically children, all fall ill.

When he was lucid, Jung described the scenes
Where we're compelled to re-enact dark myths
That we can glimpse in fairytales and dreams,
As when he dreamed himself Christ The Fish.

Freud found his myth in self-analysis
Where Orpheus, née Oedipus he led
Us lost boys, naked, to our soul's abyss
—To see in flashbacks what we missed in bed.

So ask yourselves, what myth became your Fate,
What traumas drew you in to play what part,
What self-deceptions, and what hypnoid states
Determined what exactly broke your heart.

LAIUS

Freud made his father weak—the Jew who doffed
His hat to *goys* who shoved him in the street.
But all Jews had to doff their hats while shoved.
Oedipus was a boy who scoffed,

Whose mother sat at analytic meetings.
He dreamed he fucked her as he smoked cigars;
He dreamed they both were movie stars:
Sigmund, the Witch, Hansel and the Mama.

Freud's daughter Anna had no man.
His daughter Sophie died of flu.
His sister-in-law was his mistress, *nu*?
Freud and his mother played peek-a-boo

In his books, while he made his father limp
At the crossroads where he doffed his hat.
So Freud went blind when the Nazis came
And Ausch-witched his mouth for that.

THE WITCH

In Freud's Vienna no one could believe
The children they molested there could feel,
Although from fairytales they did expect
The Witch to heat up children for a meal.

What parents do, what friends of parents do,
What supers, teachers, clergy fix, explore,
Repeats itself in self-deception, war.
You know this as persecuted Jew.

Read your memories Time makes ideal.
The text is there in metaphors and dreams,
In plays, poetry, even business schemes,
In masquerades of prayers against the Real.

Our lives were spent at two, three, four,
Watching a movie, X-rated, humming
The sound track at our parents' door
—We sometimes hear it when we're coming.

For years, decades, you repeat this trauma
In myth, the fairytale of World War II;
You bring your past into the drama,
Dreaming you're gathering gold teeth, brown shoes.

DAYDREAMING

You contemplate a European lake
Where picnickers enact a comedy
Of Aryan romance: an ingénue
Eludes a subtle pass a soldier makes.

A chunky salesman, drunk and oniony,
Gooses a widow as she's dishing stew.
You're spooning chocolate mousse or German cake
Enjoying temporary sanity.

You see the agony awaiting you:
The nightmare when the 20th Century wakes
Amidst the litter of the bourgeoisie.
You see this as an analyst and Jew.

It doesn't matter what discoveries you make
About the psyche and its history.
Time and the world will have its way with you.
Yet for a moment, the future is opaque.

You're laughing with your living family.
The day is sunny and the lake is blue.

SINISTER

*after Disney and Dali**

I took the elevator up without my keys.
A shadowed man was standing at my door.
His eyes were sinister, his mouth was grim.
"I'm going home."
                "I will not let you in."

And so I took the elevator down.
Jackhammers were flying through the streets.
My building was destroyed by bullet holes.
At windows faces looked like mimes—fake grins,

Hands like the arrested or the drowned.
Clouds of locusts burst and rained blood down.
Why were we punished, why was I
—Who thought he was a good man all his life

Who didn't seek out punishment and dread?
Why was I walking like the long dead
On streets that were a landscape out of Bosch?
No one answered my questions. It got worse.

I'll spare you all the details, spare your souls.
It is an act of kindness to shut up,
To keep my mouth sewn in a scarecrow's smirk.
"If you don't let me in . . ."
                "I'll keep you out,"
Said the man whose eyes were sinister and blind.

*Dali and Disney worked together on a cartoon.

GRAVITY OF THE BLACK HOLE

Blind at first to his self-destructive drive,
The first world war would terrify and thrill him.
Likewise Freud chain-smoked cigars, although
His worried doctors told him they would kill him.

He heard the Nazi Wolf banging down doors
But closed his eyes with smoke to keep alive
Mentally, though he elegantly described
The gravity of the Black Hole—The Death drive.

Like Christ, Oedipus, Dionysus,
Freud played the role Fate cast him in.
Biology, not intellect or art
Can counteract destructiveness within.

Otto Rank who is now anonymous
Called it The Birth Trauma, where we put to sleep
Unconscious meanings in the rhyme tomb/womb.
So, the pull toward Mommy brings us six feet deep.

The mystic quest for light inside the dark
Witch's wood always is doomed to fail.
Heroic in our search for mother's milk,
We find poison in the Holy Grail.

So we must cherish every nanosecond
And not turn Paradise into a hell—
Public in war, private in neurosis—
But live in every nonmalignant cell.

2. Snow White / Sleeping Beauty / Cinderella

FAIRYTALES

Storytellers know what scholars learn
That we in time, because of time, must burn
And to the womb of Death we must return.

Fairytales tell us what we can't forget;
That we are always children, to expect
The witches' woods of trauma and neglect.

In almost every fairytale we've ever heard
We children can't be seen, can't say a word,
And know our Fate must always be absurd.

For instance, when the father suffers grief,
He sends us children to our stepmom's double
Who puts us on a cross or *bas relief*.

Our task, then, is to be resurrected
By challenging the unexpected,
To re-appear the fractally perfected.

Hansel and Gretel, Snow White are the best
To learn from, learn never to trust or rest
—The poorest of us and the wealthiest.
When we toast Life, remember we're Death's guest.

THE PRINCE FINDS SLEEP

Why was he in the witch's woods alone
In winter, no birds singing,
Searching for love from a bygone era,
The sun gone, the snow getting colder
For his horse, the falcon on his shoulder
—When rescuers need rescuing the most?

SNOW WHITE

Her face is now a zero of despair
Over aging, money, the fatality
Of menopause, sexual schemers . . .
She lifts a wisp of gray hair
And tries to grin, "Bring me no more dreamers."

Now is her final chance to meet The Prince.
"My inner wars are over, I need *peace*
Not the poison of my mother's 'No!'
I've wakened to the dreaded five oh!

"Hurry, Prince, soon I will be bleeding.
Time brings one down incalculably slow.
My heartbeat's rapid, terrified of giving.
Like hers, hers, hers!
Hurry, Prince. I'm so tired of living."

THE PRINCE

In this fairytale of rescue we know well,
No one speaks of the Prince and what he's giving
—His confidence, his courage, and his hope

Despite his journeys through his inner hell
—His fire-breathing Sis who couldn't cope
With masculinity and independent living

—Like Pop who would debase his youthful hope:
"Your sacrifice will make your sister well.
Watch me with Mom who's never unforgiving."

So here's Snow White, apparently not living.
Behind her glass, she doesn't look too well.
Yet the Prince still has the innocence to hope

He can resuscitate her with this kiss he's giving.
Warmed by the fire in her inner hell,
He doesn't hear her cackle,"Your breath's smoke,"

Or see the Mother Witch inside her unforgiving,
Or the Victim shouting in the mirror, "I can't cope!
This Prince here thinks I'm actually living?

"He doesn't know I'm happiest with dopes,
My seven ex-s with their dwarfish living.
"I'm happiest, poor Prince, when I'm not feeling well,

"For I was fed red apples plucked from Hell.
I can't digest your antidote of giving:
Your confidence, your courage, and your hope!"

The Prince thus lonely, maddened, learns to cope.
And, though he doesn't feel or look too well,
To stay alive he constantly keeps giving
While over him she knots a zero rope.

THE SPACE DWARF'S ADVICE

I used to bang my head against a wall
To feel my self when I was growing small.
Snow White would burn herself with cigarettes
To cauterize her borderline upsets.

There are small compensations that we make
To ward off what sick upbringing will take
From us. Remember the Witch's magic
Makes what first seems homey turn out tragic.

If you repeat these homilies enough,
You'll make your nurslings sensitive and tough,
So they can turn the madness in their genes
To hope and love like Disney's closing scenes.

THE EROS DWARF

If we could tease Thanatos from her soul,
Like light—impossible!—from the black hole;
If we could root the Witch out, roast her dead,
Then you'll see Snow White raise her lifeless head.

Miracles happen, although not for us
Who were tall sons of Dionysus
Before the witches tore him limb from limb
And midget-sized us for the Brothers Grimm.

Maybe the hapless innocent Snow White
Will, like an idealized Pre-Raphaelite,
Waken from the collective dream of folklore
Which keeps her mere cliché, dead metaphor.

THE BITTER DWARF

We're merely helpful since we can't admit
That life is sex, aggression, and romance,
Determined by genetics and mere chance,
And that sheer power turns all good to shit,

That we must act with all our brains and guts
Or Death turns hope and love and care to dust,
And all our steeliness becomes mere rust;
That Snow White needs a Prince with giant nuts!

We're doomed to gaze on Snow White's purple eyes,
Impotent, as she prays some Prince will come.
We're doomed to be mere witnesses, humdrum
Office workers, not adventuresome.

THE SCHIZOID DWARF

I'm isolated, even in a crowd.
I'm also glassed-in, shut away from Time.
I used to be a *bon vivant,* a man.
I didn't want to grow up, have a child,
Or want The Witch's daughter for a bride.
And so she cursed me, she reduced my size.
Mice-like and pig-like, like the Prince deep down.
Inside I'm lively, outside the witch's frown.

PIGS

One took herself to market.
Another's mind went blank.
One nibbled on roast pork.
The cleverest lost his piggy bank.
Then one built a wooden house,
Another of brick,
Another sold real estate
Made of stones and sticks.

Finally apples of knowledge
Were stuck into their mouths.
Then all lay flat and traumatized
And grew fat on self-doubt.

MICE

Forgetfulness is necessary, not
Attachment to pain, guilt.
So, New York City rebuilt
When Wall Street crashed at Ground Zero.

In Turner's paintings of a shipwrecked storm
You almost hear a party of the drowned
Tinkling their glasses as they link arm in arm,
Before the dance floor tilted down.

Some mistake courage for denial.
Some spend their lives on trial,
Impoverishing themselves on guile
Till they cough up blood with phlegm.

Who was the farmer's wife in Three Blind Mice?
Death in an apron running after them
—Taunting Fate like the drowned clink ice
Or the ship's bride ducks under rice.

CINDERELLA

Cinderella wore a golden dress
And silver slippers mourning doves gave.
The doves were mother-figures from a bough
That flowered on her young mother's grave.

Unless we have good mothers to defeat the bad
With love, support—internalized if they're dead—
We must return to madness, cinders
Covering us in grave dust, feet to head,

Waiting for resurrection by a prince
Or Virgin Marys we think inside us.
Or male versions we've baptized in our wombs
As Oedipus, or Christ, or Dionysus

—All playing lonely, masochistic parts
Until we see our clock hands disappear:
Cinderellas all, we collapse in ashes,
Ruining a good marriage, love affair, career.

ASHES

Cinderella had to return to ashes,
Losing herself in cigarettes and pot,
As addicts are compelled to run back home.
Ashes were her mother's burial plot.

Her mother granted wishes with her doves.
She didn't get her daughter's need to feel
Her death—denied her craziness was real,
That life and death were both the poor girl's loves.

The stepsisters were cruel but crazy too.
They hid the future in the kitchen, they
Amputated feet to fill a shoe
Like soldiers in the winter of a war

Who hide in kitchens while the building burns
And amputate their souls to fit clichés
—Not *Dulce Et Decorum Est Pro Patria Mori*,
But ashes to ashes, witches' pots to urns.

THE PRINCE'S FATHER

Everyone needs The Father for advice.
The King advised The Prince on strategy:
"The slipper is a symbol for the vagina.
So hold it lovingly and you will find her.
I've seen men frightened of the black hole,
Hiding in madness, in the witch's wood,
Who won't achieve the very thing they could:
Themselves as men in action, introspection,
Afraid of wombs, most crumple their erection
And slump and limp, preferring to jerk off,
And shun Cinderella with her smoker's cough
And turn to ashes their own little lives
And fail to turn their lovers into wives."

CINDERELLA'S PRINCE

The Prince with Cinderella was persistent.
Twice he lost her, twice he freed her from
Her own masochistic disasters,
And married her and lived forever after.
The Prince went twice to her crazy house,
Smoking cigars, riding on Fantasy,
Trusting himself, his courage; he knew he could
Rescue Love, rescue himself with Reason.
He knew he was the damned but favored son.
He married what's unconscious, what we shun.

STEPSISTERS

Princesses-in-waiting, they are passive
And do not see The Prince inside themselves.
They sleep in coffins and they wake to ashes
And can't repair what The Witch smashes;

The Witch again, inside them breathing hate,
Envy, incessant put-downs, self-destruction.
They can't accept the rider on the horse.
Instead they feast on fear, inaction, loss.

THE PRINCE AND CINDERELLA: THE ENDING

In comedies the lucky couple wed
And didn't hide but, wakened, frolicked in bed.
Sex and love are Life, repression Death.
Zen masters teach us: Cherish your breath,

Breathe in, breathe out; health isn't wealth.
It's flexibility and love of what we do,
Not say—unless we talk in rhyme
And meter where we play with Time.

Or else we're tragic, trapped in dead metaphors,
True as clichés; trapped in fairytales
Whose plots we know, whose lessons we avoid,
Winding up lonely in the witch's void.

3. Hansel & Gretel / Little Red Riding Hood

CARETAKING

Yearning for caretaking all our lives,
We seek out doctors when we suffer loss
Of parents, lovers, husbands, children, wives.
As Jews traditionally seek the Cross,
We seek out Death, and so we rhyme tomb/womb.
Freud called it, "The death instinct" after Doom
Thumped drums, boomed trumpets during World War One
When his three sons put helmets on, cocked guns.

Like children mesmerized by fairytales,
We seek out rituals—the Holy Grail
Of the white light, for instance; pathologies.
(Maybe possessiveness like yours and mine
For legs, breasts, penises, drugs, wine, and work),
Like Hansel and Gretel gobbled cakes and lies
Although they read the witch's (stepmom's) smirk.

Scientists have discovered in the womb
Fetuses play with each other, until
One dies. Some sit bewildered in a room,
Incest a sister, kneel to a black-clad brother,
Or kill a partner in a business deal,
Or screw an intern to a windowsill,
Or turn to flesh and blood what isn't Real,
Or crucify a tribe, a race, a nation.

THE GINGERBREAD WITCH

For penance we would eat their flesh,
Kill their evil and take in their good.
As children eat their parents' souls in sleep.
I tell you this as the good cannibal chef,

The witch whom on Christmas Eve you
Celebrate, building a mock-up of my house
In gingerbread, unless you are a Jew
Who suffers from diabetes or nonbelief.

And Jews we eat, the tastiest one Christ.
Every Jew since him is Jesus Christ.
Oh, I've a sense of humor—look at my teeth,
Eat my cakes, children, they're nice and sweet.

HANSEL'S ABANDONMENT

"Momma don't go / Daddy come home"
—JOHN LENNON "MOTHER"

You're left alone, you're left alone.
Disney's Dog Tramp buries his bone.
Alone in bed, alone in bed
You wish your fucking parents dead.
Blind with rage at the cross roads,
Oedipus, blind with rage, explodes.
Fatherless, Hansel in a cage
Dreams he's Jesus on a stage
—The Witch's oven, Auschwitz Hell.
Abandoned, no one acts like him so well.
Hungry, he cries and sings,
"I'll eat the waste only Death brings."

GRETEL'S MOM

I ran out of house
The world said Boo
I ran back to the house
My mother said I
I ran out of the house
The world said Die
I ran back to the house
The world said Why
I ran out of the house
The world said Who
I ran back to the house
My mother said Lie
I ran out of the house
The world said Dread
I ran back to the house
My mother was dead.

HANSEL AND GRETEL'S FATHER

At home the father was depressed from shattered
Self-esteem. He gave them chunks of bread
And took them to their stepmom's witch's woods
And, barely conscious, gave them up for dead.

If their father was rich in grief instead,
Or rich in hope, ambition, greed,
He might have sexually teased them,
Bounced them playfully on his knees.

THE FATHER SAYS

"Yes, I've nothing, so I have nothing to give.
I'm so consumed by envy, trembling, guilt,
I have to send my kids into the woods.
I can't endure to see them zestily live.
I'm Hate which I have married in The Witch.

"I couldn't take their mother's being good,
Being a poor man. Poor men envy the rich
In spirit, money, time, charm, talent, luck.
I've tossed away the flesh I couldn't fuck.

"When they were small I had confidence and hope.
I felt myself, not a boy in dread,
Not needing what's most perverse, this bitch
Who stuffs, with me, their pockets full of bread,
So we won't feel guilty, giving them up for dead.

"Children aren't evil toward their parents.
They're scapegoats, it's the other way around.
We've put them in the woods or in the ground,
Hansel and Gretel slogging from ditch to ditch.
Having no self, I've married Death the Witch."

The helplessness of children or the Jews
Makes me feel angry, weak, and vengeful.
Tell me, does it do the same to you?
It always happens when you lose a war.
You scapegoat and you practice child abuse.
All History has practiced sacrifice
On a simple altar or a single tree
Where folks enact a myth or mystery.
Visit a church whose stations of the cross
Tells you what happens when we suffer loss,
Humiliation, poverty of soul.
Christ's body and Christ's blood must make us whole.

My husband who is soft gives his children bread.
To stuff their pockets as with good luck charms.
He kneels and prays that they won't come to harm,
So he can feel less guilty; though I say,
"It's civilized to send children away,
To the impersonality of ovens,
Not to an altar where their throats are slashed.
Refining Death, we turn them back to ash."

HANSEL AND GRETEL

Hansel and Gretel, almost starving, fed
On sacramental pumpernickel bread,
Were led into a petrifying wood.
They played with animated animals
As children or the persecuted do,
Surviving but emaciated, till
They came upon a crippled witch's house,
Made of cakes and honeyed bread and candied vines.
They ravished them until the witch came out
On crutches, she said, "From the First World War."
Her mouth was black, her eyes were Nazi red.
"I'll fatten you on lies," she bluntly said,
"Which you will swallow, knowing you've no choice,"
Then led them in, and music stirred their souls,
Vases were full of roses, lilacs, ferns.
On tables were dark chocolates for their hearts.
And, though she didn't say they were, sweetbreads
She plucked from other children's guts.

They ate so fast, they quickly fell asleep.
A crescent moon gave way to Aryan sun.
She lifted Hansel, lay him in a cage
And, while he rubbed his head in disbelief,
She ordered Gretel, "Fatten him on meat,
And rice and cheese, *sacher torts*, and pie.
This mixture will make all of him taste nice:
His hands, his feet, his eyeballs, and his ears.
I'll sing for you and put to sleep your fears."
Her lullaby entranced Gretel to feed
Hansel who ate till his small stomach swelled.

But he secreted a long chicken bone
Because he knew all witches are compelled
To re-enact their evil ways each day.
He knew that in his stepmom's witch's house.
So when she'd pinch to see if he was plump.
He'd stick the bone out like a soldier's stump.

Fed up at last, the witch lit the waiting oven
And ordered Gretel to creep in and test
To see if it was getting Auschwitz-hot.
Gretel delayed. "Fatwa!" the witch exclaimed
And stuck her head in, stupid in her vice.
Gretel shoved her, bolted the oven door:
"Now howl, Mother. *We* will taste what's 'nice.'"
Strong as a Sabra, she unlocked the cage
And led her brother out, uneaten, free.
They scooped up all the witches' cakes
And brought them home. Poppa was overjoyed.
The witch he married, Tyranny, was dead.
They danced and sang and on the future fed.

NOT A FAIRYTALE

If you have ever seen a life punched out,
Not in the abstract but the Real,
You'd lose your courage and your religious zeal
And realize life is not a fairytale,

A nursery of children and The Witch
(Death who in the telling always disappears),
To lull-uh-bye us as we try to sleep,
To distract us with daily cares and fears.

Always the kids return, happy and rich.
The dark woods were illusory, a film
In which the father re-appears,
Welcoming and widowed of the bitch.

A HAPPY ENDING

And there were roses in their Father's house
And cherry trees and lilacs all in bloom
And apples, peaches in its summer/spring,
A winter fire in their living room.

Time was unified and space a season
When love was resurrected like the living Christ
And Dionysus. Father had his Reason,
Teaching the lessons of the witch's woods,

Dark days of the soul
Until the soul strengthens
And what survives is what we understand:
Gretel and Hansel back home, holding hands.

ANOTHER ENDING

Now that the masks are off, the game unplayed,
The dice in someone else's pockets,
Is there nothing left to say?
Of course there is, you've lived a life.
The questions end in questions in the end.
Who was your enemy and who your friend
Matter as much as pictures in a locket
Some body left, an indiscretion, oh,
In some One's bed, in the Witch's house,
In some forgotten language no one knows.

THE WOLF'S INVITATION

"The time will come when you must disappear,"
The Wolf said, "eaten by Fate.
If you direct me to your Grandma's house,
I'll put you like a fetus on my plate.

"I'll dress up in a gown and curly wig.
I'll sprawl out like a comforter in bed
And you'll mistake my tummy for a womb
And you'll crawl in and see that I'm well-fed.

"Our greatest wish is to return to safety,
To darkness and to water like a fish.
The way is through my mouth, through my great teeth.
Just dream you're no more than a salty dish."

LITTLE RED RIDING HOOD'S BREAKDOWN

Little Red Riding Hood, traumatized,
Her mind a blank till she was sixty-three,
Grandma's age, when she was analyzed
And freed from masochistic misery

That wrecked her adult life. Although her smile
Was charming, her conscious actions kind,
Her maddening innocence managed to beguile
Sadistic men who'd help her lose her mind.

She asked to be devoured where she stood,
Offering her custard, hungry for the lie
That the wolf was Grandma, that she should
Be gullible and offer herself to die.

When we're molested at an early age,
Before our consciousness absorbs the fact
And depression strikes with repressed rage,
We suffer nightmares we must re-enact.

So pre-pubescent Little Red Riding Hood
Endured a wolf *earlier* than her tale,
A stranger in the flower-sprinkled wood
Whom she enticed, succumbed to. Later, pale,

With deep black eyes, sexually dressed in red,
Indulged by Ma as she would murderous men,
She sent the second wolf to Grandma's bed
Where he would wolf her down from feet to head.

LITTLE RED RIDING HOOD'S MOTHER

I sent her to my Mom's with custard pie.
With her breast cancer and her bad heart
She constantly thinks that she will die,
And so I've planned to give my Mom a treat.
She won't leave her gate to walk the streets
Or even to the woods behind her house.
I hate to say it, Mom's become a mouse.
When she was young, my mother was carefree, bold.
She tells me, "It's not easy getting old."
Am I just weary or a bad daughter
To speak the truth that I'm sick of hearing
Her fears of medical slaughter.
By now Little Red Riding Hood is nearing
Her gate, her house, her goddamn bed.
It's just a fairytale I wish my mother dead.

WOLF PHILOSOPHY

I have the nature of a wolf which means
I'm just carnivorous; I don't mean harm.
I'm constitutionally made of guile.
I mean to eat you, therefore, when I smile.
That doesn't make me evil, just a wolf
Who uses what in business is called "a pitch."
I'm not malicious like The Witch
Who has alternatives, like being nice.
I'm like the cat who's programmed to eat mice.

TRÜMMELBACH

A typically Swiss German, typically neat
Valley of chocolate houses with red
Raspberry flowerboxes and toy trains,
And cable cars and Heidi and Julie Andrews
Dancing among the clean sheep of the vast
Almighty mountain peaks and, almost audible
Yodeling and *glockenspieling* and *lieder*
Singing and church bells ringing: *Peace*
For Chrissakes, peace. In this
Typically Swiss German, typically neat
Valley, you stand before *Trümmelbach,*
Meaning *Streams like Drums,* before
Slopes covered with wildflowers and harp string grass,
Beneath cloud-untrammeled, serenely blue sky.
Trümmelbach. The name resonates
With romantic pomposity as you ascend
The mountain's rectum in a steep dark
Cable car. *Trümmelbach,* into whose bowels
The Munch, Eiger, and Jungfrau pour
Twenty thousand tons of glacial detritus per year.
Trümmelbach, where all boundaries are broken,
The ancient hidden shit-world of Europe,
Hitler's kingdom, the fury behind the borders
Of the Swiss dour face. *Trümmelbach,*
The bursting ethnic borders of Yugoslavia,
Of the fake Russian Empire: Georgia,
Armenia, Moldavia, Azerbaijan.
Trümmelbach, Trümmelbach, Streams Like Drums.
You walk from one bellowing waterfall,
Small Niagaras, to another, slipping, clutching the guard rail,
Staring in terror and awe, *Che Bella,*
Grand Merveilleux, Seig Heil!—Trümmelbach.

EPILOGUE

From the black hole of the womb
To the light of the birthing room,
Ticking hands intervene.
We come out bloody but clean.

From the light of Mother Earth
To the hole of anal birth
We come with the shovel's thud,
In eternal rain we track mud,

From the dark of the witch's wood
To the light of Father; good
We come, dirty and clean
And to Chaos—Mom's washing machine,

And not as Stepmom's guest.
We lie in angelic rest.
If we learn from Father now
We'll end winged and blessed,

If we fold our hands and pray
While Gretel shoves away
Stepmom who was a bad
Neglectful, abusive, mad

Witch, "Here's the devil's oven,
Begone, to your witches' coven."
I say this as a nursery rhyme.
Hopefully in Time.

So go little book from Hell
To . . . I wish you well.

II

THE TWO SIDES
OF THE MOON

God's in his heaven, all's right with the world.
—"PIPPA PASSES," ROBERT BROWNING

I'll meet you on the dark side of the Moon.
—PINK FLOYD, "THE DARK SIDE OF THE MOON"

SPRING

Philip, Billy, Roger, Bob, and Ted
Won't see this spring, or any other season.
There's not one pair of eyes among the dead.
Spring's rhythmical and rhymed, devoid of reason.
The birds are trilling bits of Bach and Brahms.
The vines are improvising drafts of psalms.
The seemingly senescent cherry trees
Open fresh flowers, pink and white and red
For our gardener listening, eyes closed, on his knees
As if they're whole notes rising from the dead.
The sky insists it's innocently blue,
That nothing happened, my friends, not to you.

THE WIDOW

She sits in silence, munching her meals.
For company she turns on the TV.
Whose presence, like the future, isn't real.
She can't imagine what she doesn't see.

Her closet is as empty as his chair.
She shuffles in his slippers across the floor
And wields his razor to thin out her hair,
But puts their sharp knives in the kitchen drawer.

Despair is in her torso, not her mind.
She has no arms. She has puppet legs.
She holds her head, as if she's ill or blind.
She stares at the phone and pleads, whines, and begs.

Her house was loud with hubbub, laughter, talk
Of actions that she can't conceive she took.
She smears cream cheese on a celery stalk
She bites before his mirror, but can't look

At how, despite her will, she's broken down,
At how her ribs are slabs of breathless meat,
At how she fears the clamor of this town,
At how the endless days repeat, repeat.

WHAT HAPPENED

What happened to Mozart who sang like a bird
More golden than Yeats' imagination wrought?
Where is Shakespeare's passionate thought,
Does his ghost pace on Hamlet's stage?
And what of Dante who consigned to Hell
His former friends who did not treat him well?
Where is Sophocles whose simple myth
Became the basis of psychoanalysis,
And Freud who smoked his mouth to death.
What happened to him, to his depth
Of soul—is it lying like a clay shard
In an earthen hole, and poor Dylan Thomas
Who ranted "Death shall have no dominion,"
Knowing he lied, or the Brothers Grimm,
What became of them, dust in sunlight
Turned like a clock—watch it long enough
And you'll go mad, or Paganini
Whose fingers danced and women swooned,
Or Gower, or Chaucer who made
Such exquisite mixes of English and French
The birds *that slepen al with open eye*
Would weep to hear the Earth took him?
What happened to Donne who would have us listen
To sermons about our limitations,
And Boccaccio, a name to stuff in your mouth
As a squirrel stuffs nuts when fall leaves redden?
What of Herbert with his convictions of Heaven
And Apollinaire, that fantastic name,
Verlaine, Villon, Baudelaire, names
That once strode Paris, and Renoir, Cezanne?
What happened to Picasso, where did he go,

And Mark Chagall who would live forever,
And Michelangelo upside down,
Painting all night like a motley clown,
And Jane Austen, so precise about the minutiae
Of interactions, where is her flesh with its intricate cells,
And Emily Dickinson who lived alone
As if time never happened?
What happened to Einstein,
His brain in a jar,
And Galileo, Copernicus, Blake?
Put them together and what do you make
Of these disappeared, where did they go?
We know but we are too timid to say,
Of Whitman who whistled his own way,
Hands in his pockets, ready to loaf,
Or Frost that dark and folksy man,
Beckett waiting in a garbage can,
All these geniuses and little you
With a pen in your hand, a nonbelieving Jew,
What of your life, where did it go?
It passed in an instant. Oh.

THE HOUSE WE HAD TO SELL

This is the house we lived in, white as a bride.
Mozart is echoing the birds outside.
We're sitting at the table playing gin.
My son is laughing every time he wins
Because he's eight, because we're all in love,
Living the future we're still dreaming of.
Spring is in the mountains, green as Oz,
In the fresh-cut flowers in the crystal vase,
Mirroring the garden where the bees are thick.
Though everyone was dying, dead or sick,
These were our uncontaminated hours,
Like bottled water sipped by scissored flowers,
Permanent in memory, sealed by the pain
That childhood ends, and we can't go home again.

THREE DIMENSIONS

The lilacs, the geraniums, a dove,
The fulsome ivy over dark brown wood,
The raucous children in a neighbor's yard,
The smell of burning frankfurters and steak.

The depth of beauty in our garden door
Frame seems immortal in this dying light.
If we could hold the present as a breathless note
A clarinetist's long *pianissimo,*

We could achieve the presence of the dove
Who perches on a young girl's fire escape.
She feeds it tidbits with a dainty hand
On which is tattooed a green wedding band.

FULLY ALIVE

My new office for psychoanalysis
Is sometimes called a Haven, sometimes Oz.
I'm going to describe it—like Frost said a kiss
Through a handkerchief translates. . . never mind.
If you were up here, this is what you'd find:

One window has an unobstructed view
Of the Empire State where no jets crash
To cover us with 9/11 ash
Infuriating this surviving Jew.
Around the corner is our major mosque
Where every lunch hour I hear chanting,
Hear chanting up and down the block.

Instead of weeping, humming, ranting
I stare at my healing Buddha, my mother's vase
Which faced her Shoah with its Chinese calm,
Stare at Steve's Assael's sketch of my son, done
Before 9/11 pulled the fire alarm,
Before Willie in *Heroism* picked up a gun.

Seagulls from the rivers West and East
Make the Empire State a roar-shock test
For those who sit up, fighting The Beast
Or lie down as I do, trying to rest
On my brown couch, over which
Is also Rick Hart's autographed print
Of the *Creation* on a church door.

Nothing here as Cooper says is *kitsch*:
Durer's print, musing St. Jerome, Steve's whore
Dressed as a nursemaid, sipping wine,
Appealing to me with a knowing squint;

My bookcase with Roger and Tony Hecht's books
Other friends' books—poetry and prose.
My father's books by Thurber and Thomas Mann
Which put my comedies and tragedies together:

Manhattan and Dark Carnival, those
Long poems/verse plays others direct and quote,
Fathering in syllabics Rexroth began
To teach me, a fat *Who's Who*
In The World for, Oh God, 1980
When Time was static.
                              Nothing weighty,
Except the bookcase, periwinkle pine,
Angels of Rick's who died in '99.

Allusions, illusions! Nothing will survive.
The buzzer rings. A patient's coming up.
I pour my coffee in my son's old cup.
The miracle of ordinary life
With my son, my office-mate my wife.
My patient enters, now fully alive.

Allusions

Steven Assael, from my point of view, is America's best representational painter.

The landscape in *Passengers* is also an illusion, the window another painting. It is from his show called "Illusions of Reality."

James Cooper is an art critic, movie critic, and editor of *The American Arts Quarterly*.

Frederick Hart's "Creation" is on the façade of the National Cathedral in Washington. His three soldiers is part of the Vietnam Memorial. Cooper has seen to it that people know how important his public art was.

Heroism is my musical drama about the uprising in the Warsaw Ghetto. "The Beast" there are the Nazis—as well as the terrorists in 9/11 that I mention in the next stanza.

The poets Roger and Anthony Hecht were brothers. Roger's work is remarkable and unknown. Tony was well-known, as was my late mentor Kenneth Rexroth.

SHAKESPEARE

If I could live a Muslim cabbie's day
Driving in traffic, parking at noon to pray
In 96th Street's Mosque, I'd stop to chat
With vendors hawking fruit, pashminas, books
Even about my centuries of fame;
If I could be a New York City hack
I'd give up every sonnet, every play,
Not in disgrace with men's eyes, not in shame
For just one sandwich stuffed with sizzling fat
Plump Falstaff in a greasy apron cooks,
I'd take back time, not scripted Fortune, back.

THE DOCTOR

Reviewing the century,
Decades of which I half-remember
Like thumbing great modernist
Poems, their rhythms
Comfortably familiar,
I stop at Dr. Williams
Who before the war
Which shaped my life
Wrote of pain, plain and simple
In his quotidian town
Where he walked
His house-calls bag
Swinging like a bell,
A stone.

RED CROSS

Dying Giants, red as autumn leaves,
Or Dwarves, white as leucocytes, form a Red Cross
How can we measure human life spans, loss?
How can we grasp what The Quintessence grieves
Or know what the primitive brain believes,
Prays to, to the Invisible above its head,
Prays for the rebirth of the almighty dead
Or understand what magic He/She pulls from sleeves?
I have no understanding anymore.
I've practiced yoga, psychoanalysis
Until I've turned into a simpleton, a bore.
We live it seems for just a mother's kiss,
A lengthy fuck from lovers and The Muse.
We take what's given, leave what we can't use.

THE POND

Nature is never wrong, the lilies say,
Simply alive in the pond, life goes on.
Despite carnivorous violence, firestorms,
We are porcelain quiet. Sit on this bench,
Listen to The Baroque Ensemble play
Music composed during The French
Revolution; cherish the bees
Closed in our petals, close your eyes,
Close them, close yourself in these harmonies.
All civilizations die.

OASIS

Dark Energy, Quintessence, God's black glove
Like the unconscious full of hate and love
Expands the universe as Einstein thought.
Dark matter, ten times matter, and has wrought
Rhythms with Gravity like rhythms in art
The macro beating of our new God's heart,
Shuttling back and forth like the preconscious.
Einstein and Freud were smarter Jews than us,
Though others perished in the Holocaust.
Another waits for us if Israel is lost
To medieval crazies at a well,
For God to rise as if he's back from Hell.
"You love life we love death," some say.
Dictators and terrorists won't go away.
We all live on the oasis of our Earth.
Let's celebrate in shuls, mosques, churches birth.

IMMORTAL VERSE

Red giants and white dwarves, and then the Witch's Broom
Nebulae, were found once Hubble began to zoom
Into the dark energy of the universe.
And you think of writing immortal verse,
Like Traherne, Herbert, Hopkins, Donne
Wrote about God?
                   Higgs Boson is fun,
The God particle which accounts for mass.
Watch the universe's "Great Wall" pass.
It's thirty million light years away.
So you write about fairytales,
Asteroids around us making brilliant trails?
Write something earthy, have something to say!

APOLOGY FOR DARK ENERGY

The dark energy with which I write
Before morning, night after night,
Creates a poem, a book of poems, what's that?
You sleep for safety curled up like our cat.

AS TIME GOES BY

That was a golden age in which we lived.
Each day was summer, God was everywhere,
In every molecule of New York City air
When we were young and just believed in us.
That was a haloed age in which we lived,
Late twentieth-century summer, love was everywhere.
I'd stop beside you on our walks to stare
At you, buying a peach, climbing a bus's stair.
And there were buts, but always and & and
Sitting in Central, doodling each other's hand,
And I recited poems, my simple fictions
In meter, rhyme and New York City diction.
As dusk drew near we'd hold a darkening kiss.
When you're distressed, you must remember this.

DELACORTE'S CLOCK

("Delacorte's chiming. It is sunset . . .")

My son is my age when I wrote that line.
When we were eating crap and smoking still.
Now for the moment we are sunset-fine.
What once was comic now is pluck, luck, will.

Hand in hand we walk toward the chiming clock.
And watch the metal animals as we did then
About to move in circles once again.
Except we're tragic and our plot is stock.

Girls in dashikis, hajibs, boys tattoos
Line up for tickets to the park's real zoo.
It's sunny still. The park's September green.
We know that what we're seeing we have seen

In different dialects and different styles.
Delacorte's clock's new melody is off,
Postmodern. We walk under it. You cough.
We plop on a bench, facing a tourist aisle

Where a jazz band: sax, drums, bass
Play *Take Five,* circling with cocaine grace.
We swing dance though we've walked this park for miles.
A gorgeous nun in blue hi-fives and smiles,

Then skips away, swinging long worry beads.
She's hooted by two ugly juveniles,
"Fuck me," they laugh. "Fuck *you,*" I say. You lead
As the band plays on for quarters, nickels, dimes.

I drop five dollars. "Wow, in these hard times!"
We walk on past an aged children's clown,
A gilded mime determined to survive
This deep recession, this expensive town.

A bum snorts, "Ain't it great to be alive?"
We edge away from him to tan our faces.
Two Russian tourists talk like mental cases
On cell phones with attachments to their ears.

But we'll hear nothing in the coming years!
You take my hand, we squeeze to death our fears.

TOY STORY

It's Father's Day. I'm seventy years old.
To celebrate, we see *Toy Story 3*,
Wearing as I did at seventeen
A blind man's 3-D glasses to watch the screen.
The theater on this summer day is cold.
So is the story about mortality.
I take my glasses off—"Why, Dad?"—to see.

The seventeen-year-old is off to school
And sadly gives his superheroes to
An old age home for toys (as you won't do),
To boys and girls, the audience's age
Who laugh at Cowboy Woody—he's Time's fool.
The other toys, friends, wind up in a cage,
Think Woody's tragic trying to escape

Time as we can't do at the next stage.
No one I know, even those who are ill,
Believes that Time like stars, those gaseous balls,
Determines, charts our silly free-for-alls
For no one bends space's fabric to our will.
Though this seems just a comedy for kids,
No one had a childhood like we did.

When you were seventeen, you joked with me,
"Hey Dad, wake up. Childhood isn't Heaven.
You aren't forty-six. I'm not eleven.
I'm off to college." "No, I don't believe this,"
I joked back, trying not to cry.
The movie ends, I have to take a piss.
Woody is given to a girl of seven.

A play of ours that's done, a poem that's read,
A night of making love, a children's park,
A television flickering in the dark,
A boring rainy Sunday afternoon
Are all that differentiate us from the dead
Who tell us both in dreams, "We'll see you soon."
We talk about our memories through the night.
You try to comfort me. I hold you tight
Till one of us falls asleep. The other can't,
Is too afraid to take a sleeping pill.
The other wakes from nightmare in a pant
And says that time is stronger than our will.
We had so many years of being ill.
Be thankful just for sleeping through the night.